Every something is an echo of nothing.
– John Cage

Ziggy Hanaor   Cristóbal Schmal

Life
(AS WE KNOW IT)

We know this much is true.

We ~~know~~ think this much is true.

We ~~know~~ think this much is ~~true~~ a truth.

In the Beginning.

In the Beginning, which was not a beginning, because time did not exist, everything in the universe was concentrated in a single point smaller than the point on this page.

And then this singular point exploded into time and space and matter.
And the Universe was born.

This is called the BIG BANG.

Dust swirled and swirled until in places it joined and became a new thing. A thing that was held together by a powerful force.

This force is called GRAVITY.

5 billion years ago, our planet was born.

A billion is all the dots on this page times a million.
If you counted from one to a billion, it would take you 37 years.

If you counted to five billion

it would take you 158 years.

Our planet was a ball of roiling, boiling, molten rock and it orbited a star we call THE SUN.

Gradually, this heaving, bubbling planet began to cool. A crust formed on top and a blanket of toxic gases surrounded it. This blanket is called: THE ATMOSPHERE.

The asteroids carried ice to the planet's surface, and the cooling planet filled with water.

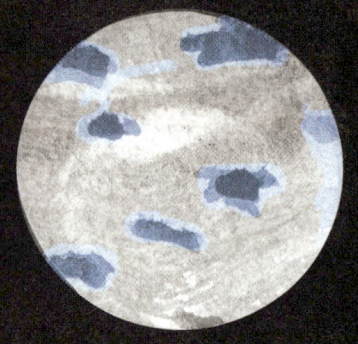 

And in the water, a miracle occurred. This is not something we understand. This is not something that can yet be explained.

This is the miracle. In the water, tiny cells grew that breathed and reproduced.

These tiny cells were ALIVE.

And when they stopped being alive, they were DEAD.

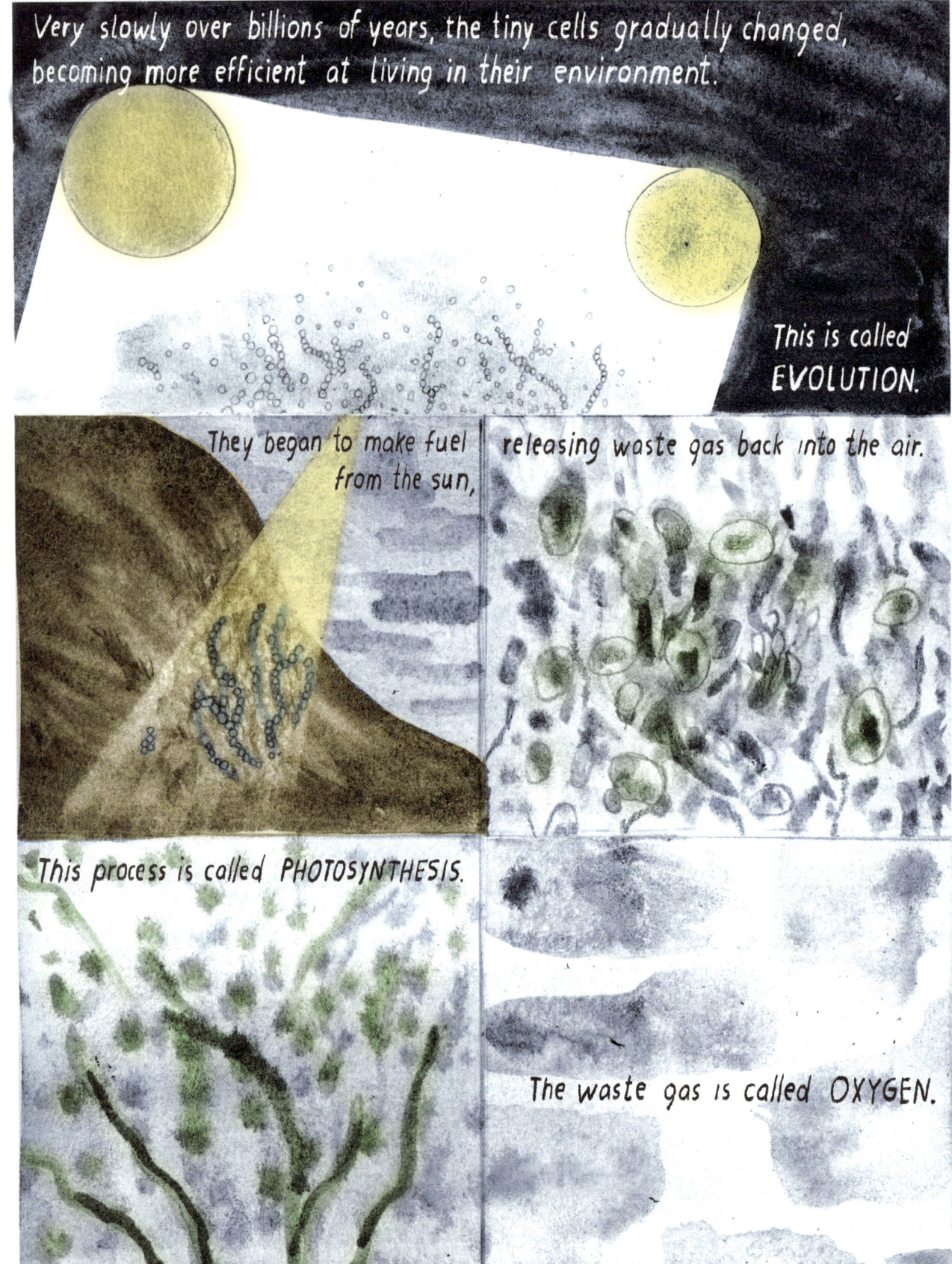

The atmosphere filled with the oxygen released by the tiny cells.

And then.

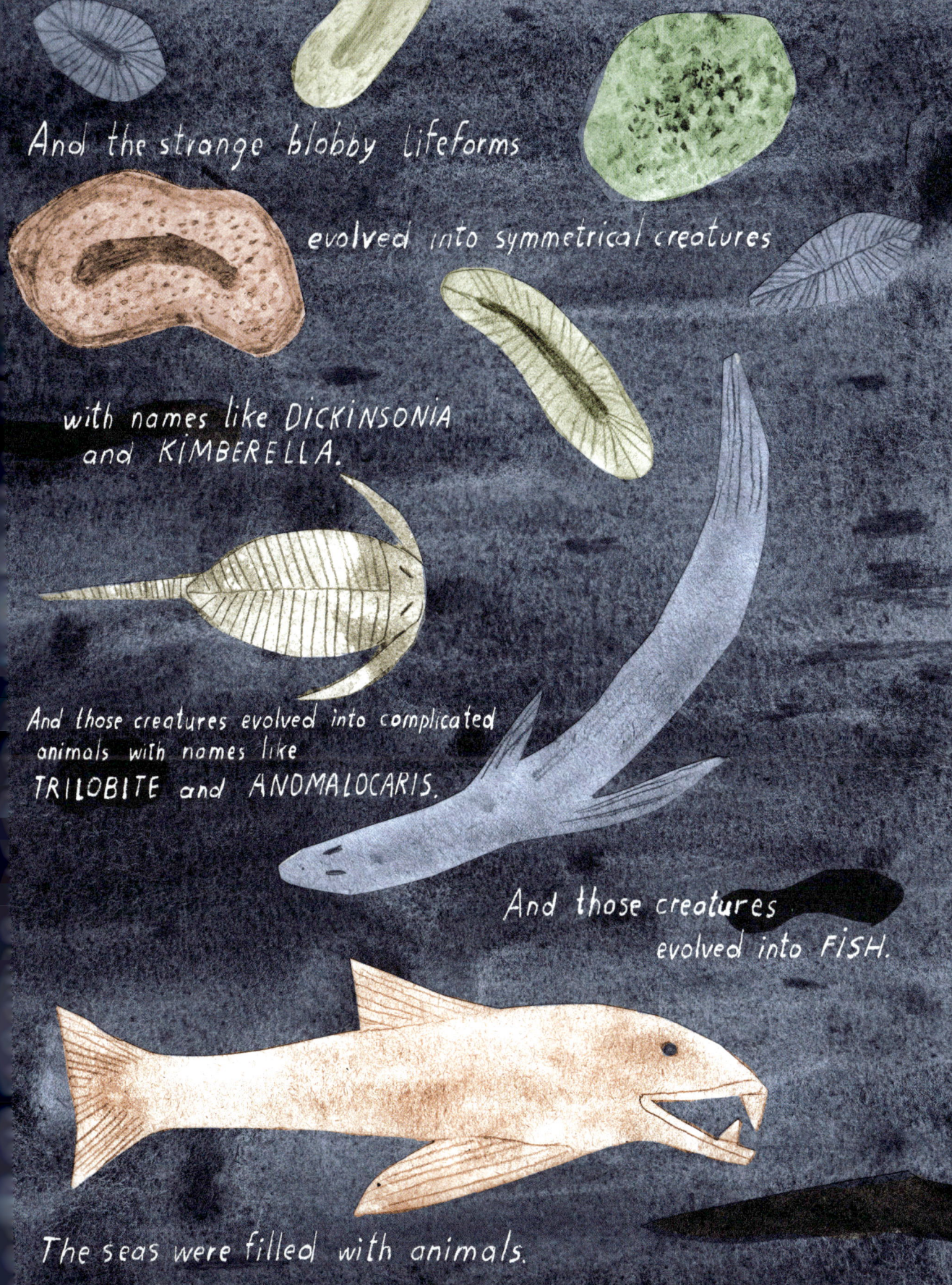

The Earth's plates shifted. Huge volcanoes erupted, pouring molten rock from the core of the planet out onto its crust.

The atmosphere turned toxic and all life died.

Almost all life.

The seas rose and the seas fell, and the atmosphere cleared itself and life returned. Some of the surviving reptiles grew and evolved into ARCHOSAURS and some archosaurs evolved into DINOSAURS.

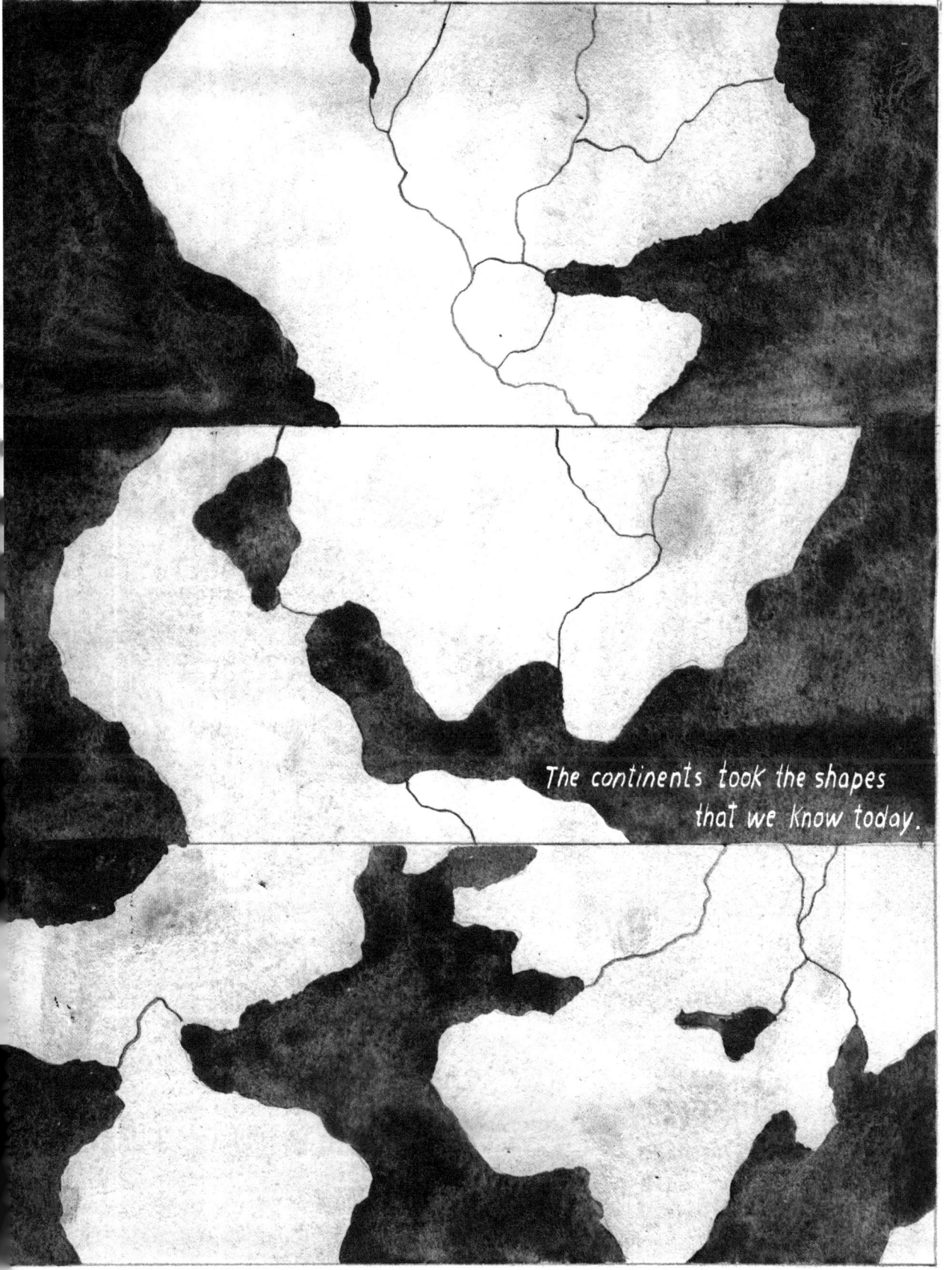

The dinosaurs grew bigger and bigger. There were millions of different dinosaurs. Some dinosaurs ate giant plants.

And some dinosaurs ate the dinosaurs that ate the plants.
Some dinosaurs grew feathers and beaks and wings.

Other animals also evolved. Some grew babies inside their bodies instead of laying eggs.

These are called MAMMALS.

And then, 65 million years ago, a giant rock crashed into the planet. This rock is called a METEOR.

It came from outer space and it hit the crust of the planet with so much force that a dust cloud blocked out the sun for years.

Without the sun, the plants could not eat. Without the plants, the plant-eating dinosaurs could not eat.
And neither could the dinosaurs that ate the dinosaurs.

Most life on the planet was wiped out.
This is called the K-T EXTINCTION.

They inhabited both land and sea.

They had hair to keep their bodies warm. They breathed air. They gave birth to live young and fed them with milk that they produced in their own bodies.

They looked after their babies and taught them things.

Some mammals lived in trees. They had flexible hands to help them swing from branch to branch. They were social animals with big brains.

These are called PRIMATES. Big primates with no tails are called APES.

The world grew very warm, and then it grew very cold.

The mammals adapted and changed in order to survive.

Five million years ago, one species of ape began to walk upright. It could see the world around it. Its arms were free to use tools.

This species is called HOMINID.

The hominids roamed in packs. They learned to communicate simply at first and then with more complexity.

But the smart ones survived. And had more babies. Who had more babies. Who grew smarter and smarter and smarter.

300,000 years ago, a new species of hominid appeared.
It had the biggest brain of all.
It could communicate not just with a small pack but with a giant tribe. It could outsmart even the biggest and most terrifying predator.

They told stories and then they worked together to make some of those stories real.

They found rhythms of living that were faster than any that had come before.

And new things happened to the planet. Not because of the volcanoes that erupted (although they continued to erupt). Not because of the Earth's plates shifting (although they continued to shift), but because humans made them happen.

They cut down forests for wood.

They traded shiny rocks with each other.

They dug up fuel that had been hiding deep in the earth for hundreds of millions of years.

They burned the fuel to stay warm and to move places and to make things.

The other animals couldn't keep up with the powerful humans and many died out.

And next?

The changes will keep happening.
The atmosphere will warm.

But the Earth will continue spinning.
It will keep going round and round the Sun.

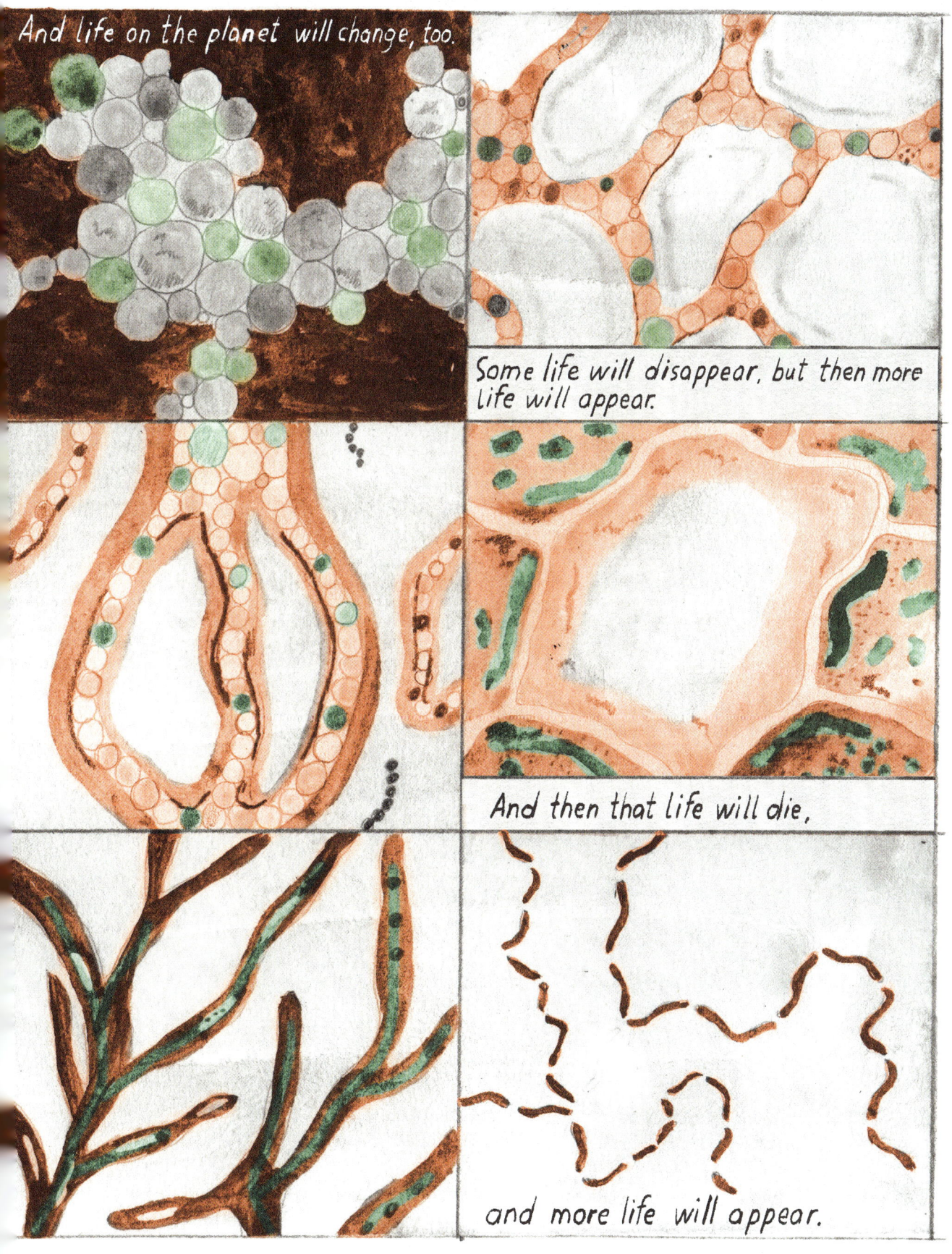

This is a story.
We think this much is true.
But we don't know for certain.

Because some things
don't make sense.

Like the tears in the fabric
of the universe
called black holes,

where nothing can exist — not even light.

And the tiny particles of matter
that somehow appear in
two places at once.

And we wonder whether there are
infinite universes.

Whether the light that shines down from stars that haven't existed for a billion years is the light that fed a planet just like ours.

Or nothing like ours.

Filled with life as we know it.

Or life as we don't.

For my cousin, Mike.
(Z.H.)

To the brightest stars Johanna, Carlotta and Vigo.
(C.S.)

LIFE (As we know it)

Text by Ziggy Hanaor
Illustrations by Cristóbal Schmal

British Library Cataloguin-in-Publication Data.

A CIP record for this book is available from the British Library
ISBN: 978-1-80066-056-4

First published in 2025

Cicada Books Ltd
Unit 9, Cliff Road Studios
5 Cliff Road
London, NW5 1UE
www.cicadabooks.co.uk

© Cicada Books Ltd, 2025

All rights reserved. No part of this publication may be reproduced stored in a retrieval system or transmitted in any form or by any means; electronic, mechanical, photocopying, recording or otherwise, without prior permission of the publisher.

Printed in Poland on FSC certified paper.